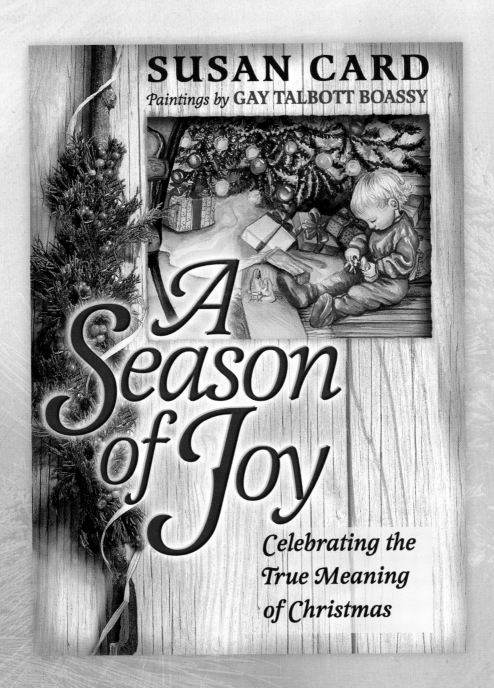

SUSAN CARD

Paintings by GAY TALBOTT BOASSY

A Season of Joy

Celebrating the True Meaning of Christmas

HARVEST HOUSE PUBLISHERS
Eugene, Oregon 97402

Many thanks to Carolyn McCready and everyone at Harvest House Publishers for their time and effort in the production of this book. Special "thanks" to Terry Glaspey for creating the momentum necessary, for great editorial insights, and for his special contribution in "Bringing the Christmas Story into Our Lives." Merry Christmas to all!

Susan Card

A Season of Joy

Copyright © 1999 by Susan Card
Published by Harvest House Publishers
Eugene, Oregon 97402

Library of Congress Cataloging-in-Publication Data

Card, Susan. 1960-
  A season of joy / Susan Card : paintings by Gay Talbott Boassy.
        p.   cm.
    ISBN 0-7369-0110-8
      1. Christmas—United States—Planning. 2. Holiday Stress—United States.
    3. Simplicity—Religious aspects—Christianity.   I. Title.
    GT4986.A1C37   1999
    394.2663 ' 0973—dc21

                                                           99-21704
                                                           CIP

Artwork designs are reproduced under license from © Arts Uniq'®, Inc., Cookeville, TN and may not be reproduced without permission. For information regarding art prints featured in this book, please contact:
      Arts Uniq'
      PO Box 3085
      Cookeville, TN 38502
      1-800-223-5020

Project Editor: Terry W. Glaspey

Design and production by Garborg Design Works, Minneapolis, Minnesota

Figures pictured on pages 22, 32, and 48 hand carved by:
      Micki and John Grosser
      1816 N. Linwood Ave.
      Appleton, WI 54914
      Ph. 1-920-739-8987 Fax 1-920-739-3574

"Light of the World"/Michael Card/Mole End Music/ASCAP. ©1982 Mole End Music (admin. by Word Music, Inc.). All rights reserved. Used by permission.

"In Stillness and Simplicity"/Michael Card (BW/ME). © 1988 Birdwing Music (ASCAP)/Mole End Music (BW) (ASCAP) (admin. by EMI Christian Music Publishing). All rights reserved. Used by permission.

"The Promise"/Michael Card (BW/ME). © 1987 Birdwing Music (ASCAP)/Mole End Music (BW) (ASCAP) (admin. by EMI Christian Music Publishing). All rights reserved. Used by permission.

"Shepherds' Watch"/Michael Card (BW/ME). © 1991 Birdwing Music (ASCAP)/Mole End Music (BW) (ASCAP) (admin. by EMI Christian Music Publishing). All rights reserved. Used by permission.

"Immanuel"/ Michael Card (BW/ME). © 1987 Birdwing Music (ASCAP)/Mole End Music (BW) (ASCAP) (admin. by EMI Christian Music Publishing). All rights reserved. Used by permission.

Scripture quotations are from: the Holy Bible, New International Version®. Copyright © 1973, 1978, 1984 by the International Bible Society. Used by permission of Zondervan Publishing House; and the King James Version.

Printed in the United States of America.

99 00 01 02 03 04 05 06 07 08 / I P / 10 9 8 7 6 5 4 3 2 1

Contents

Christmas Is Coming

It is Christmas in the heart that puts Christmas in the air.

W.T. ELLIS

I ALWAYS EXPERIENCE A TWINGE of anticipation when the first frost appears and colder weather sets in. The harvest moon has come and gone as the leaves change color and begin to die. Something in me changes as well and I come alive with excitement. Call it "the Christmas spirit" or whatever you will, but the coming of Christmas has an effect on me that goes to the very core.

The Christmas season is special for me, perhaps my favorite time of the year. My expectations are always high. I find myself spending more time indoors as the weather turns colder and feel a fresh desire to make my home a reflection of the season. I dig out our Christmas music, bring the big box of decorations down from the attic, begin to encourage the children to write down their Christmas wish lists, and start to look forward to the first snowfall of winter. In the evenings we bundle up with cups of hot chocolate in front of the fireplace and read our favorite Christmas stories.

It is not just my home that takes on that Christmas feeling. Even the stores assume a festive aspect. I am always eager to begin the search for Christmas presents, hoping to find just the right gift for everyone on my list—the kind of gift that lights up their eyes and brings a smile to their face. Christmas is a time that makes me think about how very much I love my family, and how grateful I am to God for all the wonderful gifts He has given us. It is a season of warmth, of celebration, of peace. It is a season of joy.

I stood next to the car, fumbling for my keys while the snow gently fell from the night sky. The parking lot of the mall was well-lit by lampposts decorated with garlands and by the delightful little Christmas lights that adorned the welcoming shop windows. The faint strain of a Christmas carol escaped from within the shops as people bustled in and out. I smiled, listened intently for a moment, then

The Promise

The Lord God said when time was full
He would shine His light in the darkness
He said a virgin would conceive
And give birth to the Promise
For a thousand years the dreamers dreamt
And hoped to see His love
But the Promise showed their wildest dreams
Had simply not been wild enough.

The Promise was love
And the Promise was life
The Promise meant light to the world
Living proof that Yahweh saves
For the name of the Promise is Jesus.

The Faithful One saw time was full
And the ancient pledge was honored
So God the Son, the Incarnate One
His final word, His only Son
Was born in Bethlehem but came into our hearts to live.
What more could God have given, tell me
What more did He have to give?

MICHAEL CARD

recognized it as "Silent Night."

But this particular night was anything but silent. I could hear the rapid hiss of tires traveling fast on a nearby road and the honking and revving of cars jostling for position as they lined up to leave the overcrowded parking lot. I had been lucky to find a space, having been beaten by more aggressive drivers to the first two I had spotted. Once inside the mall, I had quickly realized that the cheerful, welcoming

How Our Family Celebrates Christmas

Christmas carols have always been important in my daughter Katie's life. As I lay on the hospital bed, laboring to give her birth, her daddy, her godmother, and I sang Christmas carols for her. We watched her heart rate rise on the monitor as we sang, then drop again when we stopped. She was born in the wee hours of December 23, 1997, the dearest Christmas present we had ever received. In the drowsiness of her first hours she heard (and slept through) many Christmas carols.

Now, as she approaches her first birthday and her second Christmas, I want her to be intimately familiar with these songs of Jesus' birth. So each night, her sleepy head on my shoulder, I pace the hall and sing to her "O Little Town of Bethlehem," "Angels We Have Heard On High," and "Silent Night." There are no candles, no great choir, no pageantry. Only a drowsy baby and a mother singing slightly off-key. But it is holy. God is with us—Emmanuel—and I pray that my daughter will know as she grows up that He is with her always.

Melinda Kay Busch, Littleton, Colorado

I will honor
Christmas in
my heart,
and keep it all
the year... Dickens

POST CARD

Merry
Christmas and a
New Year.

A MERRY CHRISTMAS

windows full of lights and angels and stars and teddy bears with red sweaters didn't tell the whole story. The warmth that beckoned from inside was partially an illusion. It was not the spirit of Christmas but the spirit of commercialism that was everywhere, and I sensed more stress than joy from the shoppers who filled the aisles of the stores and clustered impatiently at the checkout counters. What had happened to my wonderful little shopping expedition?

This wasn't what I had planned when I had set out to finish my Christmas shopping. I knew I had put it off a little too long this year, as it was already the first week of December, but I figured that if I was organized and planned carefully I could get it done with a minimum of hassle. I had settled down at the table with a cup of hot tea and put a collection of my favorite Christmas carols into the CD player. Then I reflected on all the precious people in our lives, listing them on a piece of paper so that I could determine who to buy gifts for. This was a bit more difficult than I had anticipated, for it was hard to decide where the list should end. There were so many people that I wanted to buy things for. But I couldn't afford to get something for them all. How would I sort out who should receive a gift and who most likely wouldn't be expecting one? Still, I scratched my head, consulted the budget I had set for myself, and made some hard decisions. Now all I had to do was go shopping.

The thought of the beautiful decorations, the smell of potpourri, the display of candy and treats, and the

> *It's a holiday fraught with peril. So achingly beautiful, with the lights twinkling and the choirs singing and the glorious story about the Child and the shepherds kneeling in the stable, and our hearts are open, full of generous and graceful feelings .*
>
> **GARRISON KEILLOR**

How Our Family Celebrates Christmas

We try to keep Christmas simple. We relax on our homeschooling and make the season the center of our curriculum. The kids decorate the house and we also let them do the decorating of the tree. We also have a lot of creches around the house and each child has a nativity set which they have made, piece by piece over the years, in Vacation Bible School.

NICKOLINA JACOBY, GETTYSBURG, PENNSYLVANIA

echo of Christmas music all brought a smile to my face. This time of the year could be so much fun! I would wear my red skirt with the matching sweater—the perfect outfit for Christmas shopping. I would take my nine-month-old daughter, Maggie, with me. It would be fun to see her eyes widen at all the sights and sounds of the season. With my gift list in hand I could get the things I needed and still have time to bask in the simple joys of the holiday.

Of course it didn't turn out that way. It rarely does. The shops were crowded with frustrated people and with surly clerks who didn't hide their irritation. And my list? Well, most of what I had planned to buy was out of stock, unavailable, or a lot more expensive than I had anticipated. My baby quickly tired of the whole adventure, and I wasn't long in arriving at the same attitude. My feet hurt, my brain and emotions were overcome by all the noise and confusion, and Maggie's diaper was leaking onto my "perfect Christmas outfit."

Standing there under that lamppost, now with keys in hand as I balanced Maggie on my hip, I could begin to see the humor in the situation. I had become so frazzled by all the preparations for

The things we do at Christmas are touched with a certain extravagance, as beautiful, in some of its aspects, as the extravagance of Nature in June.
ROBERT COLLYER

Christmas that I couldn't even enjoy it properly. I looked up at the snow, which danced gently in the lamplight. I vowed to myself that it was time to rethink the Christmas season. Had I become so caught up in all the stress and clamor of the season that I had forgotten what it was really all about?

Isn't it easy for all of us to get so caught up in trying to create the perfect Christmas experience that we lose sight of its real meaning and significance? Have you felt yourself being pulled in two directions at once?

Some of our friends had found a simple solution to the whole problem of Christmas. They had simply removed all the "secular" elements of the holiday from their family celebration: the Christmas trees, the lights, the presents, the children waiting anxiously for Santa's arrival on Christmas morning. While I understood and respected their decisions, somehow this solution didn't seem very satisfying to me. I mean, I *liked* all the creative fun of Christmas. I liked giving and receiving gifts. I liked digging out the box of Christmas decorations, each of

> *Yet the old house, the room, the merry voice and smiling faces, the jest, the laugh, the most minute and trivial circumstance connected with those happy meetings, crowd upon our mind at each recurrence of the season, as if the last assemblage had been but yesterday!*
> **CHARLES DICKENS**

which held so many memories, some made by the children years ago and now barely holding together, but still so precious and priceless. Even though the children know the true story of St. Nicholas, I liked playing the Santa game with them, of giving them something special to look forward to and munching the cookies they left for Santa as we spread their gifts under the tree on Christmas Eve. I liked turning out all the lights in the house and squinting at our Christmas tree in the dark so that each little bulb lit up like a fiery star of color. I even liked the way the stores looked when they were decorated to the hilt, festive in a way that they were not at any other time of the year.

So how could I learn to balance all this with the simple and profound true meaning of Christmas, with the story of the Child born in a manger to save this world from sin and make a pathway to intimacy with God and a better way of living? How could I teach my children the true spirit of Christmas while still allowing them to experience the excitement and wonder of the holiday? As I look back over Christmases past, I realize that I have been on a journey toward striking this balance. It has been a journey full of false starts and of wrong roads temporarily traveled, but it has been a journey toward a richer and more meaningful Christmas celebration. As a family, we are finding ways to experience the holiness of Christmas by making a clearer distinction between what is secular and what is sacred, by distinguishing between the fun and magic of this special season and the holy celebration that honors Jesus, the true Gift-bearer of the season.

> *Whatever else be lost among the years,*
> *Let us keep Christmas still a shining thing;*
> *Whatever doubts assail us, or what fears,*
> *Let us hold close one day, remembering*
> *Its poignant meaning for the hearts of men.*
> *Let us get back our childlike faith again.*
> **GRACE NOLL CROWELL**

The Carols of

Glory to God in the highest, and on earth peace,
good will toward men.

These were the words the angel choir used to announce the coming of God's Son to the shepherds in what was truly "the first noel." Ever since then, mankind has attempted to echo back to heaven thanksgiving and praise for this gift in a variety of words and melodies. Some are great hymns of faith and others simple folk songs, but all are dear to our hearts and have become a part of the tradition of each Christmas season. Indeed, it wouldn't *be* Christmas without "O Holy Night," "Joy to the World," and "Hark! the Herald Angels Sing."

From Thanksgiving to New Year's Day, Christmas music surrounds us. And some of the most joyous moments of the season are gathering with friends and family in fire-lit rooms or out in the frosty streets to sing these lovely songs *together*. We find that the best wishes of the heart are expressed as we carol: "Love and joy come to you...and God bless you and send you a happy New Year."

Christmas

ANGELS WE HAVE HEARD ON HIGH
(SECOND CENTURY)

In A.D. 129, Telesphorus, Bishop of Rome, declared that "Gloria in Excelsis Deo" be sung on the holy night of the nativity. Centuries later it is still sung gloriously wherever believers meet to celebrate the Birth. The popular tune we sing it to is a combination of a medieval Latin chorale and a French secular melody.

AWAY IN A MANGER
(FIFTEENTH CENTURY)

Sometimes credited to Martin Luther, this beautiful fifteenth-century cradle hymn soothes like a lullaby. The sweet German melody is the perfect vehicle for the imagery of "the little Lord Jesus, asleep on the hay."

God Rest You Merry, Gentlemen
(SEVENTEENTH CENTURY)

Purported to be the most popular carol in England, this little offering of Christmas cheer has been with us since the seventeenth century. Charles Dickens even used a bit of it in A Christmas Carol: "God rest you merry, gentlemen! Let nothing you dismay!" was sung to Scrooge by bold carolers through his keyhole. Carolers have loved to sing of comfort and joy ever since.

O Come, All Ye Faithful
(SEVENTEENTH CENTURY)

This famous Christmas hymn is generally recognized as the most popular of all Christmas songs. Its origin is uncertain; it may have been sung in France as early as 1700. Its first English appearance was probably at the Portuguese embassy in London (as "Adeste Fideles"). The Duke of Leeds presented it at his Christmas concert in 1785 as "The Portuguese Hymn." Canon Oakeley's translation (the one we use today) first appeared in Murray's Hymnal in 1852, and the melody was probably composed by John Wade in 1751. Regardless of the uncertainty of its beginnings, we know that we are united with other believers around the world when we offer up this timeless invitation to adore our King.

While Shepherds Watched Their Flocks

(1700) *"While Shepherds Watched Their Flocks" was the only Christmas hymn in a famous collection of hymns written for the Church of England—and out of the whole collection is the only one still in use. Nahum Tate set his words to a beautiful hymn-tune that had been in existence for over 100 years, a melody published by Thomas Estes in 1592.*

Joy to the World

(1719) *Isaac Watts did not intend for "Joy to the World" to be a Christmas hymn (there is no mention of the Christmas story in it). It appeared originally in 1719 as part of his* Psalms of David *and was intended as a paraphrase of Psalm 98. An English theologian and hymn writer, Dr. Watts shares the distinction with Charles Wesley as being one of England's greatest hymn writers. The melody that makes this great Christmas song perfect for majestic worship in church and lively outdoor caroling is from Handel's* Messiah.

HARK! THE HERALD ANGELS SING

(1739) *It is said that Charles Wesley was walking to church one Christmas morning when he heard the bells carol out Christmas joy all over the city. Inspired by the heavenly music, "Hark! the Herald Angels Sing" was written as a companion piece to his Easter hymn "Christ, the Lord, Is Risen Today." Today's version was born when Dr. W. H. Cummings put the words of the hymn together with music written by Felix Mendelssohn.*

ANGELS, FROM THE REALMS OF GLORY

(1816) *James Montgomery, editor of* The Sheffield Iris, *first published his poem "Angels, from the Realms of Glory" in his newspaper on Christmas Eve with the title "Nativity." It was published in a hymnal in 1819 with the title "Good Tidings of Great Joy to All People." Though a journalist, Montgomery was trained for the ministry and wrote over 400 songs, 100 of which are still in use today. The beautiful melody for the Christmas hymn we sing was composed in 1867 by Henry T. Smart, who, though blind, was a noted musician.*

SILENT NIGHT

(1818) *It is believed that the organ of St. Nicholas Church in Oberndorf, Austria, was in need of repair on Christmas Eve, 1818. Wanting music for the midnight service, the pastor, Joseph Mohr, went to his friend Franz Gruber, who was the church organist, and showed him a poem he had written. He asked Mr. Gruber to compose a simple melody that they might sing together later that evening. Written for two solo voices, a chorus, and guitar accompaniment, the exquisite beauty of "Stille Nacht" still touches lives and hearts with peace and calm wherever Christmas is celebrated.*

THE FIRST NOEL

(1833) *Though claimed by both England and France, "The First Noel" first appeared in print in 1833 in England. However, it had been popular in both countries from as far back as the seventeenth century. The traditional words and music of this simple folk song have not grown stale with passing years, but remain an important remembrance of the first time angels sang of the coming of God's Son.*

IT CAME UPON THE MIDNIGHT CLEAR

(1850) *The snow was falling on a cold December day when Dr. Edmund Sears wrote the words for this lovely American carol. Though originally intended as a poem, a friend of Dr. Sears insisted it be set to music. Richard Willis read the poem and composed its beautiful melody in time for Christmas in 1851.*

WE THREE KINGS OF ORIENT ARE

(1857) *Another popular American Christmas song, "We Three Kings" was written (words and music) by the Rev. John H. Hopkins, Jr. While the Gospels do not include specific details about the Magi (it does not even say that they were royal), this favorite Christmas carol gives us delightful details that have come down from legend and tradition.*

I HEARD THE BELLS ON CHRISTMAS DAY

(1863) *No one needs "peace on earth" more than those whose hearts are heavy from living with war. Henry Wadsworth Longfellow wrote a poem entitled "Christmas Bells" on December 25, 1863, after hearing that his son had been wounded in battle during the Civil War. Read as simply a poem in that context, this hymn's deep and meaningful message is all the more clear. Longfellow entered the company of Christmas hymn writers when J. Baptiste Calkin set his poem to music nine years later in 1872.*

O HOLY NIGHT
(NINETEENTH CENTURY)

What Christmas collection could possibly be complete without "O Holy Night"? In France and around the world, people still flock to church to hear the majestic "Cantique de Noel" even as they did a century ago. Adophe Adam, composer of both the words and the melody, was a lover of music. Though he longed to write grand opera, it was only his comic operas and light ballet which met with success. Yet no one can argue with the success or the grandeur of this most popular Christmas hymn.

O LITTLE TOWN OF BETHLEHEM

(1868) *One December night in Palestine, an American preacher looked down on a group of shepherds watching their flocks by night just before he entered the town of Bethlehem for Christmas Eve services. This experience so touched Phillips Brooks that he wrote about it in a poem and asked the children of his Sunday school to perform it. Dr. Brooks asked his friend Lewis Redner (who was the choir director and organist for the church) to compose a simple melody for the children to sing. The week before Christmas came, and still Redner had not found the right tune. It is said that the Saturday night before the performance he awoke and heard angelic music, which he quickly jotted down. He insisted ever afterward that the melody to one of our favorite carols was "a gift from Heaven."*

WHAT CHILD IS THIS?

(NINETEENTH CENTURY) *Another beautiful Christmas lullaby, "What Child Is This?" was written expressly for the melody of "Greensleeves" by William Dix. It is another example of how old carol tunes often originated in popular folk tunes reaching back hundreds of years (the original melody had been first published in 1580). Centuries later Sir John Stainer arranged it to match Dix's charming verse, and a new Christmas carol was born.*

Christmas in the Heart of a Child

The holly's up, the house is all bright,
The tree is ready, the candles alight,
Rejoice and be glad, all children tonight.
P. CORNELIUS

CAN YOU REMEMBER what Christmas was like when you were a child? Can you recall the feeling of wonder and the sense of magic that seemed to suffuse all of life during this time of the year? Did you believe in Santa Claus? I did. With my whole heart. I knew the story of Jesus' birth, and I believed in that miracle. But as a child, there was something special about Santa.

I was intrigued with Santa and felt him to be integral to the celebration of Christmas, along with Jesus. The good thing about Santa was that you could occasionally glimpse him at the department store or be assured of his reality by the bundle of presents he left behind after his yearly visit on the night before Christmas.

I'll never forget the Christmas when that changed for me. It was the Christmas we moved to England.

My father was in the military, so reassignments were not unusual. I remember waking up to the warm Kentucky sun streaming in through my grandparents' farmhouse window and knowing that in just one week we would be leaving the Kentucky farm to begin a new life in a new country. This can be kind of scary when you are only six years old. As I lay in bed for a couple of extra moments, I felt the now-familiar feeling of apprehension creep over my body. What would it be like? Would I ever see my grandparents again?

Would I be able to make new friends? Would life ever be the same?

A week later, as our plane left the ground, the feeling of fear returned. But this time it was accompanied by a sense of expectation, of curiosity about what our new home would be like. Dad had gone on ahead of us to secure lodging, so I was anxious to see him again as well. It was a long flight for a small child, so I fell asleep before we had even reached the edge of the Atlantic Ocean.

When I awoke it was with the realization that our plane was descending toward Heathrow Airport in London. Pressing my face against the window, I saw stone farmhouses and the familiar sight of pastures dotted with sheep. But from the moment we stepped off the airplane I was surrounded by the unfamiliar. The cold English climate was much more brisk than the warm humidity I was used to. I would soon learn that the strange but prevalent smell that hung in the air came from the smoldering of coal fires which heated a majority of the British homes.

Our new house had one of those coal fires. It was in a charming neighborhood in a cul-de-sac made up of identical houses. The only thing that distinguished these brick homes from one another was the color of the front door and the side gate. Our door and gate were a delightful blue color—the kind of blue you find in a child's set of tempera paints.

My family's initial response was to smile at the quaintness of the pretty little houses all in a row. Over the next weeks we found plenty of other things to smile about: the strange pronunciation of words like *garage* and *vitamins,* the odd names for familiar objects (the trunk of the car was called a "boot," for example), and the wonderful little customs that were new to us (having the

On Christmas day, when fires were lit,
And all our breakfasts done,
We spread our toys out on the floor
And played there in the sun.

The nursery smelled of Christmas tree,
And under where it stood
The shepherds watched their flocks of sheep,
All made of painted wood.

Outside the house the air was cold
and quiet all about,
Till far across the snowy roofs
The Christmas bells rang out.

But soon the sleigh-bells jingled by
Upon the street below,
And people on the way to church,
Went crunching through the snow.

We did not quarrel once all day;
Mamma and Grandma said.
They liked to be in where we were,
So pleasantly we played.

I do not see how any child
Is cross on Christmas day,
When all the lovely toys are new,
And everyone can play.

K. PYLE

milk delivered to our door by the milkman and buying produce from a traveling "green grocer"). We grew to like almost everything about England. Except the cold. It was a pervasive and bone-chilling cold that could not be escaped by going inside. No matter how much coal we put in the furnace, it never really seemed to get warm enough in the house.

Of course there was one good thing about the cold winter weather. It made me think of Christmas. We had only been in England for a few weeks and

How Our Family Celebrates Christmas

This past year we have experienced some changing of traditions—some for the better, some with pain. I have given this some thought and have come to some conclusions about traditions and the inevitable transitions which must also come.

Traditions, for our family, have been the glue that holds the years together. They focus us with anticipation and excitement. Some traditions have been handed down from other generations; some we have created ourselves. They help us remember and they become for us and for the next generation a Narnia-like lamppost so that we never quite lose our way. I must confess that I have become very comfortable in and dependent on these traditions—sameness is much easier than change.

Transitions, on the other hand, impose upon us, often reminding us of our stubbornness and our weaknesses. They point out our dependence on "anchors" of our own making. But they, like traditions, also become lampposts. They point us into the past to look at how God has cared for us. As we refocus and sharpen our understanding, the lamppost also illumines the new path God sets us upon. I believe that traditions strengthen and sustain us and bring us joy in living. But the heaven-sent transitions conform us to the image of Christ and bring us to an abiding sense of peace in the knowledge of His presence and His faithful promises.

MEREDITH AND CHRISTY FLAUTT, FRANKLIN, TENNESSEE

already Christmas was upon us. The very thought made me feel warmer inside, despite the cold!

The days leading up to Christmas were very busy, and yet I wondered when Christmas would ever arrive. My mother signed me and my siblings up for the church choir, where we would sing carols in the Christmas Eve service and get to dress in robes just like those worn by the members of the adult choir. At school we made crafts and at home we helped Mother make cookies and opened the numbered windows of our Advent calendar. One by one the windows opened, marking the days as we drew nearer to Christmas. The decorations came out of storage, the Christmas tree went up, and we hung our stockings in anticipation of Santa's arrival.

The Christmas Eve service was very special. Mother made us take extra care to dress in our best clothes and look neat. There was never any question of the importance and solemnity of this night and what we were gathering together to celebrate. When it came time to sing the carols, it was with great passion. "Away in a Manger," "Hark! the Herald Angels Sing," "Joy to the World," and "O Little Town of Bethlehem." Our choir sang loudly and with as much sincerity as our little hearts could muster. As I sang, I envisioned the images that accompanied every song. I saw the angels hovering over a small barn. I smelled the hay and felt the roughness of the manger. I heard the animals and saw the shepherds gathered around the newborn baby cradled in Mary's arms. During the last song, we were entrusted with candles, holding them tightly and away from our bodies so as not to burn our hair or someone's clothing. When the minister pronounced the amen, we quietly filed out of church and headed

> *Help us rightly to remember the birth of Jesus, that we may share in the song of the angels, the gladness of the shepherds, and the worhsip of the Wise Men.*
> **ROBERT LOUIS STEVENSON**

27

How Our Family Celebrates Christmas

Our family has a special tradition in gift giving. Taking our pattern from the Magi (gold is precious, frankincense is a perfume, and myrrh is a burial spice), we have grouped our presents into three categories: Precious (like gold), Frivolous (like perfume), and Practical (like burial supplies).

JOHN TUITELE, PEORIA, ARIZONA

home for the next big part of the Christmas celebration: a visit from Santa Claus.

When we arrived back home from church, it was cold in the house, as usual. As Dad came in the door, he joked to Mother that it was so cold they would be forced to build a fire and he was worried Santa might not be able to come down the chimney. I was horrified. "No, Dad! Please, Dad, don't build a fire!" I begged. I could not shake from my mind the image of our great benefactor going up in flames as he tried to descend our chimney. It was only after wresting Dad's solemn assurance that he would not build a fire on this of all nights that I could calmly climb the stairs to my bed.

But I still couldn't sleep. I worried aloud to my siblings that I hoped Santa realized that we had moved and knew where our new home was. Then we talked about what we each hoped to find under the tree and rubbed our socks together to make electricity (we always wore socks to bed in England). Finally, we quieted down and began, one by one, to drift off. That's when I heard it. It was faint, but distinct: the sound of sleigh bells on the roof. I knew instantly that it was the sound of reindeer. I strained to try to hear other sounds, but the night was too quiet and I fell asleep. When I awoke in the morning, I found confirmation of Santa's visit under the tree: just the very presents I had asked for.

Not many days later, my older sister and I were playing in the front yard with a neighbor. When I asked her what Santa had brought her for Christmas, she gave me a condescending look.

"Santa's not real," she smiled in amusement. "How old are you? I can't believe you *still* believe in Santa Claus. I've known he wasn't real for a long time."

"That's not true!" I shouted, coming to his defense. I looked to my older sister for confirmation, knowing that she would put this foolish child in her place. My sister hesitated a moment.

"It's true, Susan," she said gently. "It's really Mom and Dad who leave the presents."

I was stunned by this revelation. How could this be

true? In a moment, some of my childish innocence disappeared and I found myself having to rethink my whole view of reality. *So this is reality,* I thought to myself. *This is it. There is no real magic in the world.*

At that moment, some of the magic of Christmas was irretrievably lost. I could still hold onto the story of Jesus' birth, but the demise of Santa left a hole in my Christmas celebration. Something magical and fun was gone.

As an adult, I

Christmas . . . is not an external event at all, but a piece of one's home that one carries in one's heart: like a nursery story, its validity rests on exact repetition, so that it comes around every time as the evocation of one's whole life and particularly of the most distant bits of it in childhood.

FREYA STARK

To Wish you a merry Christmas

RAFAEL SANZIO
MADONNA SIXTINA, DRESDEN

Christmas Greeting

A Merry Christmas

© Gay Talbott Boassy

don't believe Santa has godlike qualities, but see him instead as our culture's rendition of the famous bishop St. Nicholas, who lived centuries ago. But I have come to believe in the deep magic of Christmas, of something special this holiday holds for us if we are willing to reach out and accept it. Though the world's reality intrudes into the celebration, it doesn't need to rob us of a deeper sense of wonder and amazement. Seen in this light, Christmas can become a time of unusual beauty and magical joy. It can truly be a special time of the year. And this reality

I had three fine rosy-cheeked schoolboys for my fellow-passengers inside .... They were returning home for the holidays in high glee, and promising themselves a world of enjoyment. It was delightful to hear the gigantic plans of pleasure of the little rogues, and the impracticable feats they were to perform during their six weeks' emancipation from the abhorred thraldom of book, birch, and pedagogue. They were full of anticipations of the meeting with the family and household, down to the very cat and dog; and of the joy they were to give their little sisters by the presents with which their pockets were crammed.

WASHINGTON IRVING
Old Christmas

has nothing to do with Santa Claus.

There is no reason why, as adults, we have to throw away the joy that we can find at this time of the year. Let us enter into the celebration with our children. Adults don't get much chance to play in the course of their busy lives, but there is no reason why the kids should have all the fun. There is no reason why we can't keep some of that wide-eyed wonder we had as children alive in our hearts. If we begin to focus on what Christmas really means, we will find an even deeper cause for celebration and joy.

31

Simplifying the Season

Once I am truly convinced that preparing the heart is more important than preparing the Christmas tree, I will be a lot less frustrated at the end of the day.

HENRI NOUWEN

MY HUSBAND, MICHAEL, is a singer and songwriter. He struggles to get just the right thoughts down on paper—words that clearly express the things he is passionate about. Once he has finished a song, I have the unique joy of being the first audience for his new

When God gives us a gift, He wraps it up in a person.

DR. WILLIAM LANE

creation, its first listener. I remember the winter he was working on songs for his album *Present Reality*. We were only a few days away from Christmas, and he had been working hard on the new record. He had been gone all morning, holed up in his office with his pen, his Bible, and his guitar. When he walked in the front door, I could immediately sense his excitement over his newest set of songs.

I particularly enjoy listening to music outdoors, where the beauty of nature can accompany the beauty of the music. So I grabbed my Walkman and inserted the cassette Mike had recorded for me, as I headed out the door. It was a chilly, wintry day, the snow falling softly and piling up around the trees which surrounded our property. It was so completely quiet that the only sound I could hear was the crunching of my own boots in the snow. I pushed the "play" button. The first song on the tape was enjoyable, with a powerful spiritual message. But

when the second song started, it stopped me in my tracks. Over the gentle melody, played simply on his guitar, came these words:

> In stillness and simplicity
> In the silence of the heart I see
> The mystery of eternity
> Who lives inside of me
> In stillness and simplicity
> I hear the Spirit's silent plea
> That You, oh Lord, are close to me
> In stillness and simplicity.

As the words tumbled forth and the snow settled gently onto the landscape, I sensed an awakening within myself. This peacefulness, this calm, this quietude were filled with meaning. *This* was the spirit of Christmas. It was the simple message of God's peace in our heart that reflected the Christmas spirit. Not all the hassle and stress, the commercialism and the noise, but the stillness of knowing that God is with us and that He cares for us. He did not come to us with blazing trumpets or a

Shepherds' Watch

Shepherds watch, listening to lambs bleat
Tired backs, worn out and cold feet
All life long living like outcasts
All life long, longing for life.

A dazzling light, the voice of an angel
Gripped with fear, terrified they fell
One like a man, yet awesome and holy
A face so fierce and yet strangely kind.

"Do not be afraid, I've good news of great joy
Your Savior has come, He's Christ the Lord
As a sign to you the One born today
Will be wrapped in rags, asleep on the hay."
And all at once the air filled with angels
Glory shone, of holiness they smelled
"Glory be to God in the highest
And peace on earth to those He loves."

MICHAEL CARD

loud public proclamation, but in the quiet reality of a baby born in a stable 2000 years ago.

This was the Christmas spirit that I knew I wanted to foster in my home. And I realized that it must begin with me. I needed to make some decisions, though. And I knew that some of them would be hard ones. I needed to ask myself what kind of Christmas spirit I was modeling in my home. Was I so concerned about everything being "just right," and making certain that everyone was perfectly happy and pleased, that I put forth an attitude of stress and frustration rather than the simple joy of celebrating Christ's birth?

After I packed the gifts and my child into the car at the end of one particularly frustrating shopping trip, I still had one more stop to make on the way home. I had to pick up the dogs at the veterinarian. As he handed over my

How Our Family Celebrates Christmas

When I was a child I was usually bored by 10 A.M. on Christmas morning. The living room was strewn with paper, I'd played with all of my new toys (and broken two), I'd worn out one set of batteries, and I sat in the midst of it all—bored. As an adult I wanted to put the focus of Christmas on Jesus and give a different emphasis to giving. Therefore, our Christmas celebration starts on Christmas Eve and runs through New Year's Day. Presents may be given at any time throughout that stretch of days. For example, I'll surprise Mom by putting a new sweater (with a bow) in her sweater drawer, where she will find it within a day or two. This makes giving more fun.

MARTY MILLER, LAWRENCE, KANSAS

dogs, he made the mistake of asking me how my Christmas shopping was going. Without intending to, I found myself pouring out some of my frustration at the day I had had and at the whole

Christmas season. Christmas had become much too complicated. "You know," I said, "the problem with Christmas is women."

Now I might have been offended if those words had come out of *his* mouth, but I think most women would agree with me. Men, for the most part, take a much more laid-back approach to the season. In many homes, their role seems to be little more than climbing up on the roof to hang the lights! But women seem to spend countless hours worrying about making everything just right. We have all been influenced by books and magazines filled with pictures of gorgeous homes meticulously decorated for the holidays. Yet these can either inspire us or intimidate us. If we go to them to get some good ideas that might be fun to make part of our celebration or decorating scheme, they can be very inspiring. But if we look at what someone else has done and feel defeated because we could never find time and energy and money to dress our home up in that manner, then it can be very intimidating.

Suddenly, it is not enough to give a meaningful gift. It has to be wrapped in such a way that it is a work of art. You cannot just wrap paper around your present and stick on a bow. Everything has to be perfectly coordinated, beautifully designed, and make a personal statement of originality. It is not enough to cook a simple, delicious meal for Christmas dinner. It has to be a fabulous gourmet concoction that is healthy at the same time! It must please the eye as much as the palate. And our tree? It can no longer be a collecting place for festive clutter. It must now be seen as a fashion statement in home decor. The tree must be coordinated with other decorations and give evidence of all our abundant creativity. In fact, I think we even can get a little competitive with each other about whose tree is most beautifully decorated and who can bake

> *Let go of the unrealistic expectations that besiege you. Keep Christmas preparations simple and rewarding.*
> **SANDRA BOYNTON**

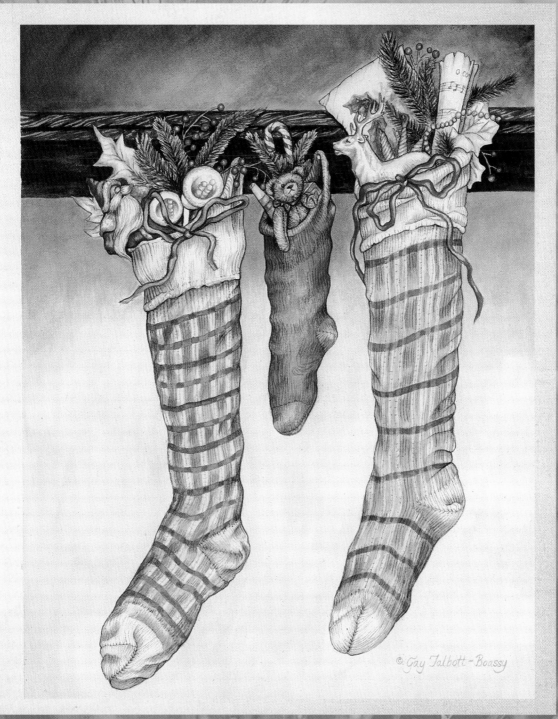

37

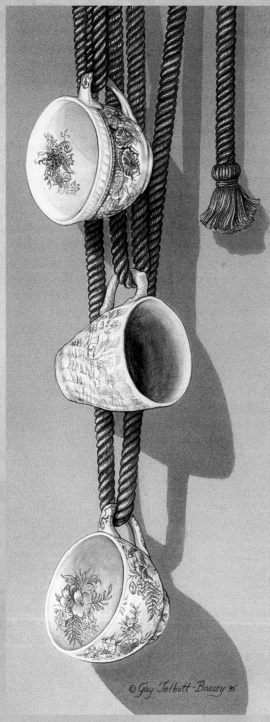

the most cookies. But Christmas isn't a contest.

All this comparison robs us of our contentment and of our simple joy in the season. There is no way we can live up to the models of Christmas perfection we see in magazines. After all, real families don't live in those photographic homes. Or, if they do, I would like to see them a few days after the pictures were taken, when the kids have engaged in a game of hide-and-seek around the tree or the cat has climbed its branches in search of something to play with.

After all, what do we really want in our tree? A work of art? Or a collection of ornaments that sparks great memories? I've decided that my trees don't have to be perfect. Instead, they are a reminder of the continuing wonder of Christmas and of all the special Christmases past. Quite honestly, many of our ornaments are not pretty. They are pieces of family history. There's the one made out of green construction paper which is topped by a red bow and has a picture of Maggie cut out and pasted to it. Another is a piece of square cardboard covered with different styles of macaroni glued haphazardly with Elmer's glue and spray-painted gold. This one was the creation of my son, Will. I doubt that anyone else would get excited about hanging these ornaments on their trees. But to me they are precious treasures. When I look upon them I see a six-year-old girl with a missing tooth and a toddler who had as much glue on his hands as on the ornament. And isn't that what we really want to be reminded of?

Wedded with the pressure that everything be beautiful is the pressure to make everything fun. Wives and mothers sometimes feel like we are responsible to be the engineers of Christmas joy, that it is up to us to fulfill everyone's expectations and desires. But no matter how

> *May you have the greatest two gifts of all on these holidays; someone to love and someone who loves you.*
> **JOHN SINOR**

much we want to do it, we can't. Christmas does not have to be a performance that we orchestrate. Instead, we should reexamine our priorities so that Christmas can be as joyful, as restful, and as focused on its true meaning as possible. It should be a time of relaxation and concentrating on the deep things in life that we can be thankful for: family, friends, and especially the love of God.

So what are some practical things we can do to simplify the season? How can we remove some of the pressure and focus on what really matters? I do not claim to be an expert or someone who has it all together. I'm still struggling with these issues myself. But I am committed to making some

ongoing changes in the way I celebrate Christmas. Here are a few ideas that are working for me:

Ask yourself whether all your traditions are really necessary. A couple of years ago I realized that sitting down to write out all my Christmas cards had become an overwhelming task. My list had simply become too long, and with

all the demands of my small children, I couldn't find the time to make my Christmas cards meaningful. So instead of continuing to stress out over the expectations I had placed upon myself, I decided to take a break for a few years

from this particular tradition. This doesn't mean I'll never send another card. It just means that I had to weigh out the cost of the stress in my life right now with the impact of deciding not to send cards. Making this decision has given me more time to focus on things that are important to me and my family.

Rethink your approach to gift-giving. I love to find the *perfect* gift, but usually that is impossible! I think that we have come to put the wrong emphasis on our giving and receiving of Christmas gifts. We've loaded ourselves with the burden of trying to get the perfect gift for everyone on our list and forgotten that the paradigm given by the Baby in the manger is that we must give ourselves as the present. I wonder if we try to create too much of an impact with the presents we give, to try to create heaven on earth for the recipient by giving him or her just exactly the right thing. Can you remember the times when you prowled up and down the aisles of the local department store in agony over what to get Uncle Charlie or Aunt Ethel? A nice, thoughtful gift wouldn't do. It had to be something that would send them into fits of joy. Problem is, you realize you have no idea what they would really like. Still, if you look long enough and spend enough money, maybe...

This is the wrong way to look at gift-giving. After all, isn't the real purpose of a gift simply to say, "I appreciate you"? One idea that has worked for us is to pick out one gift that has meant something to us during the year and give that to most of the people on our list (excluding, of course, close family members and our dearest friends). Oftentimes it will be a book. This year we gave copies of a book on prayer to everyone on our list. It is a book that both Michael and I found helpful, so we wanted to share it with others. By giving a gift like this, we are not so much trying to meet everyone's need as we are sharing something of ourselves with them.

I have also learned to keep my eyes open for gifts all year long. When I run across something that I think would be "just the thing" for one of the kids or one of my closest friends, I go ahead and buy it—even if it is only March. Then, when December rolls around, I find that a good deal of my shopping is already done.

Finally, we have found as a family that the most enjoyable kind of gift-giving is that which meets the needs of others. It is such a joy to give to those who are less fortunate, who may lack some of the basic essentials (or near-essentials) of life. As a family, we like to use some of the money we might spend on ourselves and give it to families who don't have as much as we do. Whether it be

> *The problem with our gift-giving is that we take something humanly meaningful and try to make it divinely meaningful. The stress of making an impact on someone's soul via a physical object leaves us feeling strained and empty.*
> **KEN COPE**

sending an offering to a missionary family, taking the name of an underprivileged child off a giving tree, or targeting a family whose resources are slim, this kind of giving reflects the love that God wants us to share with everyone. Many organizations stand ready to help you in this process during Christmas.

Consider the issue of time. Have you noticed how quickly the calendar fills up as we draw closer to Christmas? December 25 looms as the absolute deadline. By then, every bow must be tied, every ornament hung, all the tinsel put into place. Before that date we have so many wonderful opportunities: parties, get-togethers, activities, visits to relatives and friends and neighbors. If I'm not careful, I can find myself committed to something just about every evening. And though it's all fun stuff, even too much fun stuff can be a source of tension. I've learned the necessity of saying no, of making difficult choices about how busy I really want to be during the Christmas season.

When I really think it through, the most important thing to me is spending time with my family during the holidays. I have to make some solid decisions to block out time with them, or all the other activities can quickly crowd out our time together. For example, one of the things I love to do with my children is to bake Christmas cookies. Now I know that this will take a considerable block of time and leave the kitchen looking a mess, but it is worth it to me. So is having a number of evenings alone together as a family during the holiday season. If that means I have to say no to some other activities, then that's what I do. We only

> *The Christmas message goes straight to our searching hearts and tells us that Christ alone can bring us lasting peace— peace with God, peace among people and nations, peace within our hearts.*
> **BILLY GRAHAM**

have so many hours. We must make wise decisions about how to use them.

These are only a few suggestions. What works for my family might not work for yours. You may make completely different choices. But the important issue is that we find ways to relieve some of the stress surrounding Christmas so that we can experience the real joy that comes from the true meaning of Christmas. Not only that, but we can find more time for what really gives us the most joy: sharing Christmas with our family. When you learn to simplify the season, you'll find yourself less stressful, with more time to spend together and to make the kind of lasting memories that you'll cherish your whole life long.

How Our Family Celebrates Christmas

One of our more unusual traditions has to do with Christmas stockings. In addition to the others, we hang one up with Jesus' name on the cuff. During the Christmas season we put money in it. Several years ago, my husband decided that we would match whatever was the highest dollar amount spent on a present and put it in Jesus' stocking. In addition, all our children donate money to the Jesus stocking.

Then, after Christmas, we decide where to send the money. One year it was to a missionary, another year it was to friends that had financial problems. Interestingly enough, one year we found a $50 bill in the stocking that none of us had put there. A few friends know about our tradition since the stockings hang in our living room, but we never did find out who the mystery donator was!

LESLEY WILLIAMS, SEATTLE, WASHINGTON

Our Favorite Christmas Books

Every Christmas we find at least one new Christmas story to add to our family library. Throughout the month of December we read one of these treasures together every night. Reading aloud together gives us some special time as a family and an opportunity to reflect upon what the season means. Here are a few of our family favorites:

MICHAEL HAGUE'S FAMILY CHRISTMAS TREASURY BY MICHAEL HAGUE

A delightful collection of classic Christmas stories, carols, and poems with art-work by one of my favorite illustrators, Michael Hague. Appropriate for all ages.

THE BOOK OF CHRISTMAS EDITED BY NEIL PHILIP

All the traditional favorites are included in this collection with beautiful illustra-tions by Sally Holmes that give it a classic feel.

THE GIFT BY R. KENT HUGHES

This beautiful retelling of the birth narrative is biblically accurate and full of practical applications for our lives today. The text is brought to life by the artwork of Ron DiCianni and the calligraphy of Timothy Botts. A wonderful book for Advent reflection.

THE TWELVE VOICES OF CHRISTMAS BY WOODROW KROLL

Each chapter of this fascinating book looks at the birth of Jesus through the eyes of a different biblical character. Powerful insights come to us through the voices of Mary, Joseph, Zechariah, the shepherds, and others involved in the nativity story.

YOU ARE SPECIAL BY MAX LUCADO

This was my Christmas gift to many friends and family members last Christmas. I include it with my list of Christmas stories because it has a message that is foundational to why Jesus came in the first place: God loves us! Just the way we are!

FATHER CHRISTMAS AND THE DONKEY BY ELIZABETH CLARK

Children always seem to relate well to animals. This book tells a story about how Father Christmas meets the needs of some children and their animals.

A CHRISTMAS CAROL BY CHARLES DICKENS

This is certainly one of the most famous Christmas stories of all time and is available in numerous editions. We add more fun to our yearly reading of this book by distributing the various roles to the members of the family and reading aloud as our part comes up.

CHARLES DICKENS: THE MAN WITH GREAT EXPECTATIONS

BY DIANE STANLEY AND PETER VENNEMA

Ever since we discovered this short and readable biography of Charles Dickens, we've added it as a prelude to our yearly reading of A Christmas Carol. *It is full of marvelous illustrations which will help keep the interest of even the youngest listener.*

THE CRIPPLED LAMB BY MAX LUCADO

Lucado is a great storyteller, and this is a powerful story that illustrates the concept of strength in weakness through telling how a little crippled lamb was privileged to be in the presence of Jesus on the night of His birth.

THE POLAR EXPRESS WRITTEN AND ILLUSTRATED BY CHRIS VAN ALLSBURG

The beautiful illustrations alone were enough to capture my imagination! A delightful story about Santa Claus for anyone who once believed.

THE TWENTY-FOUR DAYS BEFORE CHRISTMAS BY MADELEINE L'ENGLE

The popular children's author tells of a Christmas season in the home of her fictional Austin family. Very encouraging and fun!

A CUP OF CHRISTMAS TEA BY TOM HEGG

A delightful little poem that reminds us to share ourselves with others at Christmas.

THE STEADFAST TIN SOLDIER BY HANS CHRISTIAN ANDERSON

One of my friends collects tin hearts to decorate her tree, since they remind her of this classic story. I cannot read it without thinking of her!

The Best Christmas Pageant Ever BY BARBARA ROBINSON

This marvelously funny story puts a lot of things in perspective for me. It reminds me of the many ways that the Christmas story touches the hearts of even the most hardened.

The Tale of Three Trees BY ANGELA ELWELL HUNT

This story is a reminder of how God can use each of our lives in small ways that are bigger than we ever could have expected.

The Gift of the Magi BY O. HENRY

You can find this short story in many Christmas collections, but don't miss the wonderful illustrations in the edition with artwork by Lisbeth Zwerger which set this edition apart from the rest. A great reminder of the true spirit of giving.

The Christmas Miracle of Jonathan Toomey
BY SUSAN WOJCIECHOWSKI

A precious story of a miracle birthed through giving. The illustrations by P. J. Lynch are unforgettable!

The Nutcracker BY E. T. A. HOFFMAN

Everybody knows the famous ballet by Tchaikovsky. Here is the story it is based upon. A Christmas tradition!

The Birth Narratives from the Gospels of Matthew and Luke

Our Christmas celebration would not be complete without reading the story of Jesus' birth from the Bible. Reading the story straight from the pages of Scripture is a must!

Embracing Our Traditions

Christmas! No other time grants us, quite, this vision 'round the tree or gathered before the fire, we perceive anew, with joy, one another's faces. And each time, faces come to mean more.

ELIZABETH BOWEN

I STOOD KNEE-DEEP in tinsel, garlands, and decorations, trying to figure out how to decorate my newly cut Douglas fir with such a touch of beauty that it would please even Martha Stewart, and with such a playfulness that it would make my children giggle with glee. How on earth could I create the perfect tree? I furrowed my brow, trying to recall all the ideas I had read about in magazines I had collected over the years. And I found myself getting more than a little bit stressed by the contemplation of how I would dress up the tree this year. And then the absurdity of it struck me. I was getting stressed out by a *tree.* I was missing the whole point of Christmas. Does this sound familiar? There's the sudden realization that your priorities about Christmas have become a little unbalanced and that the beautiful and peaceful celebration of Christ's birth you had planned for has been muffled by ho-ho-hos, silver bells, and rockin' around the Christmas tree.

> *The magi, as you know, were wise men— wonderfully wise men— who brought gifts to the Babe in the manger. They invented the art of giving Christmas presents.*
>
> **O. HENRY**
> *The Gift of the Magi*

When some Christians realize this danger, they take strong measures. Fearing the intrusion of any element into their Christmas celebration that is not specifically Christian, they have made their homes virtual Santa-free zones. But in the process of banishing Santa, Frosty the Snowman, and the

Immanuel

A sign shall be given
A virgin will conceive
A human baby bearing
Undiminished Deity
The glory of the nations
A light for all to see
And hope for all who will embrace
His warm reality

Immanuel
Our God is with us
And if God is with us
Who could stand against us?
Our God is with us
Immanuel

For those who live in the shadow of death
A glorious light has dawned
For those who stumble in darkness
Behold your light has come!

So what shall be your answer?
Oh will you hear the call?
Of Him who did not spare His Son
But gave Him for us all
On earth there is no power
There is no depth or height
That could ever separate us
From the love of God in Christ.

Immanuel
Our God is with us
And if God is with us
Who could stand against us?
Our God is with us
Immanuel

50

MICHAEL CARD

Christmas tree, they have also removed some of the fun from Christmastime for their kids. Other Christians, wanting to keep the sense of magic that surrounds the holidays, unthinkingly incorporate all the ways our culture has of celebrating Christmas. But doing this can make it easy for them to get so caught up in all the glimmer of the holiday that they can forget its true meaning.

Is there a way to keep both elements alive in the holiday season? For it to be a time of rich spiritual reflection at the same time as it is joyous and wonderfully fun? This has been an issue that Michael and I have struggled with over the years, sometimes getting a little too legalistic, other times missing the mark by temporarily losing sight of what it is really all about. But we continue to work to find the balance.

A few years ago, I attended a Christmas coffee for women. Our hostess had

How Our Family Celebrates Christmas

When my parents were alive, we used to pack all six members of the family and our two dogs into the car and travel to Florida to spend Christmas with them. After they died, we were forced to develop some new traditions for the holiday. Here's what we do now: On Christmas Eve we go out to eat at a restaurant (a real treat for a family of six), ride around and look at lights (ooh...ahh...), go to our church service, and then end up back at home to open presents. We finish off the evening with a helping of my special Christmas fudge.

GAIL PTACH, RICHMOND, MICHIGAN

created the most inviting and festive atmosphere. There were plenty of cookies, cups of tea, and good friends. While milling around, admiring the way she had decorated her home, I came across a basket full of books sitting on her hearth. When I asked about them, she said that they were there so that she could use them to help shape the experience of the Advent season for her family. One of the books that particularly caught my attention was a story about the historical St. Nicholas.

As I looked over the book, something became very clear to me. Stirring inside was a growing restlessness that I experienced every year at this time. Suddenly it dawned on me what the restlessness was all about. I realized that I was uncomfortable with Christmas because on that day we celebrated two very different events with two very different messages. There was the secular Christmas celebration of Santa and jingle bells and good cheer, which sometimes had a tendency to get commercialized. Then there was the celebration of the birth of our Lord. I felt the responsibility to try to keep them together, but somehow they resisted my attempt, like when you try to get two magnets with the same pole to join together. When I realized the distinction, I was finally able to understand the problem and get a glimpse of the solution.

Many of our traditions just don't mean the same thing to us that they did when they first started. The Santa we know today, for example, is very different from the St. Nicholas of old. He has become a largely commercialized figure, representing more the desire to receive than the joy of giving. I realized that if I could help my children see Santa through the eyes of the historical St. Nicholas, it would inspire in them positive Christian virtues such as how much fun it is to give to others. But if we ascribe too many godlike characteristics to Santa, such as omniscience (he knows everything) or the power to judge (he knows if we've been naughty or nice), then we can cloud and confuse

> *There's a dear old tree,*
> *an evergreen tree,*
> *And it blossoms once a year.*
> *'Tis loaded with fruit*
> *from top to root,*
> *And it brings to all good cheer.*
> LUELLA WILSON SMITH

© Gay Talbott-Boassy

the deepest meanings of Christmas for our children. I've found that it's possible to put the emphasis where it belongs, helping our children understand that Jesus is real, the Savior of the world, and Santa is a *game*. A fun and enjoyable game, one that can inspire a little holiday entertainment, but not the center of the Christmas season. The attitude we hope to foster is that of

for you

©Gay Talbott Boassy

54

Father Christmas in C. S. Lewis' *The Lion, the Witch, and the Wardrobe* who, pointing beyond himself, says, "Merry Christmas! Long live the true King!" At his best, Santa should point us to Jesus.

A lot of our holiday traditions are like this. If we understand them from one angle, they can be a terrible distraction from the true meaning of Christmas. But from another perspective, they can contribute to our celebration of a meaningful spiritual holiday.

Do you ever wonder where certain traditions came from? In my own search for a more meaningful Christmas, I did some research into the past in order to better understand the present. I learned a great deal. First, I learned that the battle over how a Christian should celebrate Christmas has been going on for centuries. Martin Luther wanted to avoid the celebration of any saint's day, including that of St. Nicholas. He feared the human tendency to worship the saint rather than the Savior. The Puritans were also opponents of Christmas, objecting to the secular elements which tended to overshadow the religious ones. But the other thing I discovered in the course of my study was that many traditions I looked into had hidden or forgotten spiritual connotations. Perhaps, I thought, some of these could be reemphasized to help us keep the focus on the Lord.

This set me to the task of examining our own family traditions. Why do we do what we do? When it comes to traditions, I think everyone should consider "cleaning out their Christmas closet," to determine which traditions are worth keeping and which we should do away with. We can ask ourselves questions like: What is

> *For unto us a child is born, unto us a son is given: and the government shall be upon his shoulder: and his name shall be called Wonderful, Counselor, the mighty God, the everlasting Father, the Prince of Peace*
> **THE BOOK OF ISAIAH**

55

the real meaning of this tradition? Does it point us to the true meaning of Christmas? Does the time and energy it requires keep us from having a peaceful Christmas spirit? Can we enjoy it and still stay within our budget?

It is certainly not necessary to find deep spiritual meaning in every little thing we do at Christmas. It's OK just to have fun with certain elements that have no religious content. But you may be surprised at the depth of spiritual meaning in some of our popular Christmas customs. And what joy we can experience as we learn to keep a sense of balance about it all and grow in our awareness of the meanings behind our chosen traditions.

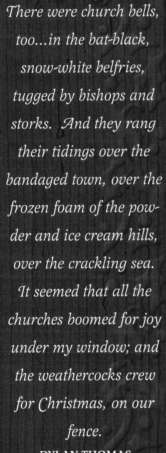

There were church bells, too...in the bat-black, snow-white belfries, tugged by bishops and storks. And they rang their tidings over the bandaged town, over the frozen foam of the pow-der and ice cream hills, over the crackling sea. It seemed that all the churches boomed for joy under my window; and the weathercocks crew for Christmas, on our fence.

DYLAN THOMAS

A Child's Christmas in Wales

How Our Family Celebrates Christmas

When our little family was just starting out, we often wondered how many gifts our children should receive. At very young ages, especially, they would open one gift and become so entranced with it that they were not interested in opening the rest. Or they would quickly open all of their gifts and push them aside, then wonder what was next, bewildered that "that was it."

Several years ago, I overheard another mom describe her family's "Wise Men Christmas," where each child receives three gifts. It sounded like a great idea, and we have been doing just that ever since.

Sometimes we have to get creative and join small, related items into one gift (inexpensive doll clothes or Matchbox cars, for example). We also have a large gift bag filled with books, CDs, and puzzles or games—family gifts—for them to open. Stockings are also separate. When all is said and done, the kids still have plenty to open (perhaps still too much!) and are quite delighted with their well-chosen gifts. We don't feel that our focus is quite so removed from the very reason we have a celebration at all. And, of course, it simplifies the shopping season, provides a stop to the purchases, and forces us to really consider the value in each thing we give them.

ANN E. HANSEN, ADA, MICHIGAN

Meanings Behind
The Christmas Tree

One of the primary symbols of the season of joy is the Christmas tree. What wonderful memories we create with our children as we tramp through new-fallen snow in search of just the right tree to take home and decorate. Or a trip to the local tree lot can be your family's traditional way of choosing the "perfect" one. We bring our newly chosen tree into the house and carefully load its fragrant branches with lights, tinsel, and ornaments, both handmade and store-bought, each one with its own unique story. How did this incredible Christmas tradition begin?

Though evergreens have been used through the centuries to brighten the dark, lifeless days of winter, the Christmas tree began as a holiday custom in Germany in the sixteenth century. While tinsel, candy, fruit, nuts, and small presents for children usually adorned its branches, Martin Luther, who started the Protestant Reformation, is traditionally credited with putting the first lights on the tree. According to a widely popular story, one Christmas Eve he was walking through some fir woods when he noticed the brilliancy of starlight reflecting off icicles that hung on the trees. He went home and set up a Christmas tree behind the nativity scene in the children's nursery and put candles on the branches to signify the stars that shone down on the Child's birth. This custom spread throughout Germany, and German immigrants took it with them to other countries.

Decorating a tree at Christmas largely remained a German tradition, however, until the mid-nineteenth century. Prince Albert, the German-born husband of England's Queen Victoria, introduced the custom to Windsor

the Traditions

Castle to give Christmas pleasure to his children. Some years later, the Illustrated London News *published a full-page engraving of an eight-foot tabletop tree with six tiers of branches beautifully decorated and with the royal family standing around it. The tree was an instant success.*

Widespread use of the tree in America is attributed to Sarah Hale, editor of Godey's Lady's Book, *who reprinted the picture of the "Christmas Tree at Windsor Castle" in 1850. By 1852 the Christmas tree was firmly established in New England and many other states.*

Ornaments for the tree had traditionally been edible confections or toys, but by the late 1800s, glass ornaments (less heavy and not as likely to topple the tree over) were being imported from Germany. Tinsel was invented in 1610 in Germany, but

until the mid-twentieth century was made of real silver and tended to tarnish in candlelight. Candles were replaced by electric light in the 1880s, which made it possible to have the tree lit throughout the season and made the tree much safer. Suddenly the old-fashioned Christmas tree was vested with new glory! (Wire hooks for hanging ornaments were patented in 1892.)

No tree would be complete without an angel or a star gracing its top. Whichever you choose in your home, they are both appropriate as announcers of the Baby's birth. Many families even place a nativity set or a manger under the tree. The Christmas tree reminds us that we all can come as the humble shepherds did that first night and worship Him. It is an ever-present invitation during the busy season to come and adore God's greatest gift.

Christmas Cards

Christmas cards...so colorful, so comforting, so encouraging, so much a part of our Christmas tradition. And yet possibly no other Christmas custom allows for change and variation as much as the offering of Christmas greetings. The carols we sing have been sung for centuries, Santa has been in his jolly red suit for over a hundred years, and our Christmas tree (though now with electric lights instead of candles) has been with us since the sixteenth century. But Christmas cards...now they can come to you by e-mail! Still, many people may prefer a less up-to-date method of communicating to friends and loved ones warm wishes for the season. "I'll be home for Christmas" may only be possible in dreams and in the form of a card your family can hold in their hands. So it needs to be special. But whether you are communicating

across the miles or just across the street with the neighbors, giving and receiving Christmas cards is a part of participating in the joy of the season.

Christmas cards only originated in the middle of the last century. Prior to that, it simply took too long to mail holiday wishes to everyone you knew. Letters in the American colonies could take weeks to arrive, and mail from England up to a year. But in the mid-1800s two things made cards at Christmas possible: the steam railroad engine and the idea itself.

Sir Henry Cole is generally credited with sending the first printed Christmas cards. In 1843 he hired J. C. Horsley to design a card for him that he could send to friends and family. He had 1000 of these cards printed and asked a shop owner, Joseph Cundall, to color each one by hand. Mr. Cundall then sold the cards Sir Henry did not use. The penny post had been instituted in England in 1840, allowing for an affordable method of sending holiday greetings. Later it became even more popular when a card could be mailed in an unsealed envelope for a half-penny at Christmastime.

Christmas cards first appeared in America a few years later. But it wasn't until 1875 that Louis Prang, a German-born printer in Massachusetts, revolutionized the Christmas-card industry in the United States. His process for printing Christmas cards was especially good—he was able to print up to 15 different colors. He also held contests each year in Boston for the best Christmas-card designs. The winners were awarded cash prizes. From that time, interest in Christmas cards swept the nation.

Christmas cards can let you share your individuality. You can choose a nativity scene, a Victorian winter scene, or a photograph of the family fishing trip last summer. They reflect the personality of the sender...one of the things that make them so special. Christmas arrives at a marvelous time—just before the beginning of a new year. What an ideal moment to wrap up the old year and start fresh with people we love by sending them greetings of love, joy, and peace on earth. It is also a great opportunity for Christians to share the true meaning of Christmas with unbelieving neighbors, relatives, and friends. What better news could we bring than to share what Jesus has done for the world!

Advent

In the United States today, we tend to consider all the days between Thanksgiving and the start of the new year as "Christmastime." But this is also the season of Advent, which means "coming." During Advent we prepare for the coming of Jesus. A "season within a season," Advent begins on the fourth Sunday before Christmas and ends on Christmas Eve. It is a time for the believer to prepare with prayer and meditation for a holy day (this, of course, is where we get the word holiday). *It can be a wonderful part of the Christmas tradition, because it is easily celebrated at home. Children love the rituals of lighting the candles in the wreath or opening the squares on the Advent calendar.*

Advent began in the Middle Ages. The return of Christ was thought to be imminent, so believers set a time apart to prepare for His second coming. Eventually it spread throughout the Western church and became a time of preparation for the nativity. There are two popular ways to mark the time of Advent:

The wreath. *A popular symbol of Advent, the wreath is a circle of evergreens containing five candles—four around the wreath and one in the center. Usually the four candles on the outside are three of blue or purple and one of pink, with the candle in the center being white. Though there are many different traditions regarding the candles, the important thing to remember is what they represent. The circular green wreath is considered a symbol for the eternal life of God. The candles are a picture of the* coming of the Light of the world.

On the first Sunday of Advent a purple candle is lit, on the second Sunday, two candles are lit, and so on. Traditionally, the third candle (the pink candle) is the candle of joy and is lit on the third Sunday of Advent. The center candle is lit either on Christmas Eve or Christmas Day. Victorian families often suspended the wreath over the table, but if you have small children, you may want it down at their level.

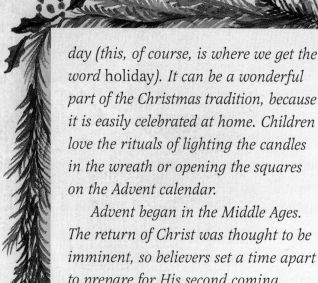

You can make each candlelighting a celebration with prayers, Scripture readings, carols, and special holiday treats. Have fun creating your own family traditions with this time of focusing on God and His gift.

The calendar. *A calendar may also*

be used to count off the days of Advent. An Advent calendar has 25 windows, each covered by a little door. Starting December 1, these doors are opened every day until Christmas Day. They might have small surprises of toys or chocolate behind them for children, or pictures from the Old Testament leading up to the time of the nativity.

Another very special and unique "calendar" is the Jesse Tree. Its branches bear ornaments that symbolize the events from the Old Testament leading up to the birth of Christ. (On December 1, for example, you might hang an apple ornament, in remembrance of the events of Genesis 3.) The name

"Jesse Tree" comes from a verse in Isaiah: "A shoot will come up from the stump of Jesse; from his roots a Branch will bear fruit" (Isaiah 11:1).

For the Christian, Advent captures the spiritual side of Christmas perhaps better than any other of our beloved traditions. Decorating the tree is a joyous time; baking, buying, and making presents create fun-filled memories; and writing notes and letters to insert in Christmas cards all contribute to the wonderful season that is Christmas. But there is a reverential aspect as well we should remember, and that is emphasized as we make room in our lives for the celebration of Advent.

Angels

Imagine that you and your friends are simple shepherds, sleepily caring for your sheep one starry night just outside the little town of Bethlehem. Then, without warning, an angel appears in front of you! He knows he has startled you because his first words are "fear not." And then he tells you he has news of great joy: "For unto you is born this day in the city of David a

Savior, which is Christ the Lord." Suddenly, the heavens are filled with an angelic chorus giving praise to God.

Angels have been a part of Christmas from the beginning. The shepherds, of course, were not the first recipients of a visit from angelic beings. The first "Christmas angel" appeared to Zechariah. He was a

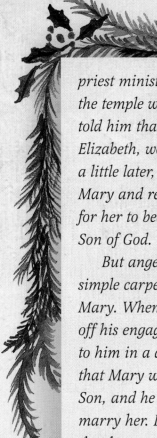

priest ministering before the Lord in the temple when Gabriel appeared and told him that he and his wife, Elizabeth, would have a son. And then a little later, the same Gabriel visited Mary and revealed to her God's plan for her to become the mother of the Son of God.

But angels also came to Joseph, the simple carpenter who was engaged to Mary. When he considered breaking off his engagement, an angel appeared to him in a dream and assured him that Mary was indeed carrying God's Son, and he was not to be afraid to marry her. Later an angel told Joseph that he was to flee to Egypt in order to protect the Child. He received yet another angelic visit when it was safe to return to Israel.

Today, images of Christmas angels hang on our tree or about the house watching over our Christmas packages and preparations. Some of our images of Christmas angels were influenced by popular painters like Michelangelo, Rubens, and Blake. They are also present in many of our favorite Christmas hymns and carols: "Angels, from the Realms of Glory," "Angels We Have Heard on High," and "Hark! the Herald Angels Sing," just to name a few.

Angels are important to the celebration of Christmas because they are the bringers of good news, those who proclaim what God has done for the human race. Like the angels, we too should lift our voices this Christmas season and give witness of God's glory and His love.

December 25

Why do we celebrate on December 25? The Bible is mysteriously silent regarding the actual date of Jesus' birth, though we can be assured that He came at God's appointed time. Though the church began commemorating the birth of Jesus fairly early

in its history, there was no unified agreement as to the appropriate date. Church fathers in Rome chose December 25 because this was the day that pagans celebrated the winter solstice in a festival called Saturnalia. By choosing this day, the church was able to transform a day of pagan celebration into a Christian holy day. And doesn't it seem right that during the time of year when it is the darkest, people everywhere can rejoice in the coming of the Light of the world?

The Poinsettia

Next to the Christmas tree, perhaps no other decoration says "Christmas" more than the poinsettia. Its beautiful red-and-green color has made it the perfect Christmas plant since 1828.

The poinsettia derives its name from Joel R. Poinsett, first U.S. ambassador to Mexico and an avid botanist. He discovered the plant while in Mexico and had it shipped to his greenhouse in South Carolina. The plants thrived and were eventually named after him. At first he only sent them to his friends, but before long they became very popular. Until the early 1900s, poinsettias were usually sold as fresh cut-flowers, but by 1923 Paul Ecke of southern California was developing a multibranched plant. This process was improved upon until 1963, when the plant developed into the form we enjoy today.

There is a Mexican legend that one Christmas Eve two small children, so poor they had nothing else to offer, brought a bouquet of weeds to lay before the image of the Christ Child during the Christmas Eve service. A miracle occurred and the weeds burst into a beautiful plant of red and green. They were known from then on as "Flores de Noche Buena" ("Flowers of the Holy Night").

What a lovely image this is of our lives...poor and "weedy" as they may be, our lives burst into beauty when humbly offered to Jesus.

Gift-Giving

"For God so loved the world that he gave his one and only Son..." (John 3:16). God, the best Giver of gifts, began a tradition one starry night long ago in Bethlehem. And some two years after the nativity, it is recorded that wise men brought precious gifts as an offering of worship to the Child. Gift-giving has been part of the celebration of His coming since the beginning! We enter into that tradition every year when we give gifts to one another.

Gifts have always been a part of the Christmas tree. When the Christmas tree first made its appearance, the toys underneath it and on its branches were generally not wrapped. However, wrapping gifts became popular in the mid-1800s and has never gone out of style. In 1917, J. C. Hall (of Hallmark) imported decorated envelope linings from France as "gift dressing." The tradition quickly caught on. Our Christmas trees would be incomplete without a pile of beautifully wrapped packages beneath them, in all sizes and colors, just begging to be shaken.

For most Americans, Christmas presents are opened on Christmas Day or Christmas Eve, but in other times and cultures the exchange of gifts often occurred on other days. For centuries European countries made December 6 (St. Nicholas' Day) the gift-giving day. And in Victorian England, Boxing Day (December 26) was developed as a day to provide Christmas boxes to servants or to the poor. January 6 (Epiphany) has also been associated with the custom of gift-giving.

Giving gifts during the Christmas season is a great way to teach your children about the joy of giving. The opportunity to offer something special to another person helps them understand that it is always more blessed to give than to receive.

Hanukkah

During the same time of the year that Christians celebrate Christmas, Jews celebrate Hanukkah, also known as the Feast of Dedication. It begins on the twenty-fifth day of Kislev on the Jewish calendar and lasts for eight days. During the celebration, menorah candles are lit and placed on window ledges to remind the world of the miracle that God performed during one of the darkest times in Jewish history.

When Antiochus Epiphanes ascended the throne of one of the kingdoms of Alexander the Great, he began a campaign of terror and persecution of the Jews in Jerusalem. The low point of the persecution occurred when he desecrated the sacred altar of the Jewish temple by sacrificing pigs and other unclean animals on it. This was simply too great an outrage to be ignored. A Jewish man by the name of Judah the Maccabee led a rebellion against the Greek oppressors and was able to defeat them.

When Judah and his followers returned to Jerusalem to reclaim the temple, they found it stripped bare of all its gold and the precious items used for holy ceremonies. Judah encouraged the people of Jerusalem to come together and refurbish the temple, which they did with gladness. After its restoration, they had a ceremony to rededicate the temple once again to the God of Israel. The ceremony was to last eight days, but they only found enough consecrated oil to last one day.

Miraculously, with this limited supply of oil, the candles burned for eight days. Hanukkah is a remembrance of this event and a celebration of the God-sustained light given to His people following a very dark period of their history.

There are two reasons that Hanukkah should be of interest to Christians. First, all of Jewish history has a special significance for the believer, as it is foundational to our understanding of how God works, even in the present day. Second, it is of interest because Jesus used this very feast as the stage for communicating an important truth about Himself. Just at the time of the year when Jewish homes were

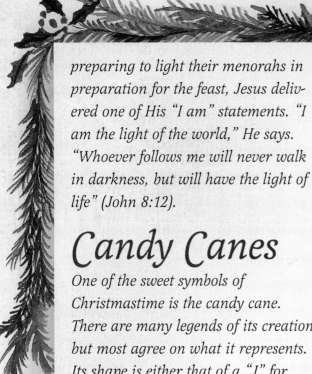

preparing to light their menorahs in preparation for the feast, Jesus delivered one of His "I am" statements. "I am the light of the world," He says. "Whoever follows me will never walk in darkness, but will have the light of life" (John 8:12).

You are the light of the world, O Lord,
And you make your servants shine,
So how could there be
Any darkness in me
If you are the light of the world?

MICHAEL CARD

Candy Canes

One of the sweet symbols of Christmastime is the candy cane. There are many legends of its creation, but most agree on what it represents. Its shape is either that of a "J" for Jesus or a shepherd's crook (Jesus is the Good Shepherd). The candy's hardness represents the fact that Jesus is the Rock of Ages. The white stripe represents His virgin birth and purity, and the red stripe is for the blood He shed for us. The peppermint is in the same family as the hyssop, an herb used in the Old Testament for purification and sacrifice.

Thinking on these things helps us to see that the candy cane is much more than just a seasonal treat. It is another image of Christmas—not of Santa but of the Solid Rock, the sinless Son of God, and of the sacrifice He made so that we could share eternity with Him.

Santa Claus

Santa Claus is one of our most popular and endearing images of Christmastime, but the jolly old elf we know and love has only been around since about the middle of the nineteenth century. The original gift-giver and stocking-filler is generally recognized to be St. Nicholas.

According to legend, Nicholas was born in the village of Patara in Asia

Minor about A.D. 280. At 19 years of age, he was ordained a priest in the Christian church and later became Bishop of Myra, a city near Patara. He was known far and wide for his good deeds and generous nature. Soon after his death (December 6, 343) he became St. Nicholas. He was recognized as the patron saint of many different portions of society, especially of sailors and children. Stories began to circulate about how he suddenly and miraculously appeared to those in need, and even filled the stockings

of the poor while they slept. It wasn't long before children began to celebrate his name day (December 6) by hanging their stockings the night before by the fire. Sailors carried their belief in St. Nicholas all over the world, and soon peoples of many European countries were forming their own Nicholas Day traditions of good deeds and gift-giving.

In the early 1600s, Dutch colonists to America brought with them their version of St. Nicholas (Sint[e] Klaas or Sinter Claes). The British presence in North America introduced Father Christmas. But by

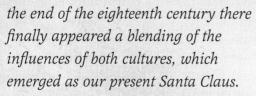

the end of the eighteenth century there finally appeared a blending of the influences of both cultures, which emerged as our present Santa Claus.

Clement Moore's "A Visit from St. Nicholas" ("The Night Before Christmas") is generally credited for changing the appearance of the tall, thin bishop into the roly-poly, cheery image we have today. In verses he originally penned only for the amusement of his children, he described a figure sneaking into his home through the chimney with a big sack on his back. This strange person, whose round little belly "shook, when he laughed, like a bowl full of jelly," was depicted as twinkling, merry, and white-bearded. A family friend sent a copy of Moore's poem to her local newspaper, which first published it on December 23, 1823. Over the next few years "A Visit from St. Nicholas" was widely published by many newspapers, and by 1860 it was probably the best-known Christmas poem in the United States.

Thomas Nast, a famous political cartoonist, drew extremely popular pictures of Moore's Santa for Harper's Weekly from 1863 to 1886. These cartoons of Santa and his workshop at the North Pole helped to create for us over a century ago our present fairy-tale-like representation of what was once simply a good and generous man.

The joy of these and other Christmas traditions comes from finding ways to make them your own, of creating your own unique traditions to celebrate and enjoy the season with your family. Let me share three traditions that have become especially important to our family celebration.

Several years ago, we began to use an Advent wreath. We found it a nice way to get the family to start focusing on Christmas well in advance of the actual day. It also provided a consistent reminder of the real significance of the Christmas season. Although an Advent wreath normally has only five candles, a friend of mine has one with 25 candles. This is especially fun, because you can light another candle every evening and accompany it with a family devotion. By Christmas night, you have a beautiful spiral of candles, each one progressively smaller. There is something special about children and candles. My kids love candles, which seem to create an unusual sense of reverence in their hearts when they see them.

Another tradition that is important to our family is reading Christmas books. Over the years we have amassed quite a collection. We love to gather together in front of the fire and read aloud from some of the great Christmas children's books, short stories, and poems. The children lean forward in suspense, lost in the unfolding tale, while Michael and I revel in the joy of the familiar pleasures we get to experience all over again. On pages 44 through 47 in this book, you'll find a list of some of our family holiday favorites.

But probably our most unique and spiritually satisfying tradition is our yearly trip to the barn. Because of our love for the Lord, we wanted to find a way to help our children enter into the realities of the Christmas story. So every Christmas we go to a real barn, using only lanterns for light, and read aloud the Christmas story from the Bible. Without fail we are always moved to remember what Christmas is really all about and how, from that humble beginning in a barn, God began something which has changed our lives for all eternity.

These are just a few of the things that we do. With a little creative thought, you can think up new ideas for how your family can celebrate this season of joy!

Bringing the Christmas Story into Our Lives

Love came down at Christmas;
Love all lovely, love divine;
Love was born at Christmas,
Stars and angels gave the sign.

CHRISTINA ROSSETTI

I HOLD THE CHRISTMAS CARD in my hand, gaze at its depiction of the nativity, and say to myself something like, *Now this is what Christmas is really all about.*

It is a scene I have seen reproduced so many times. Under a clear winter sky, a couple takes shelter beneath the roof of a stable usually meant for cattle. But it is warm there, a soft glow from somewhere lighting the tableau of a mother and father gathered around a straw-filled manger. The look on the faces of the new parents is one of deep peacefulness and contentment, as the animals crowd near for a glimpse of the newborn child. A small cluster of shepherds are on the scene as well, accompanied by an angel who had brought them the "good tidings of great joy"—news of the birth of the Christ Child. Somehow the angelic figure floats in the air above, his motionless wings seemingly unnecessary to keep him aloft. Perhaps the sheer joy of the message he brings is enough to help him

Christmas is a blessed season, and if we come to it seeking the warm, confirming Spirit which testifies of Jesus Christ...we will find light and life in the experiences of this holy day.

BARBARA B. SMITH

overcome the force of gravity. A single star shines high in the heavens. One perfectly symmetrical beam streams forth from it and falls upon the scene. Perhaps this is the source of the un-earthly light. All in all, it is a scene of wonder and peace.

But perhaps the first Christmas wasn't as pretty or tidy as a Christmas card. Let's not forget: He was born in a barn (or at least the first-century equivalent). And let's remember that this stable (or was it just a cave hewn out of a rock?) was normally home to any number of animals. The smell that pervaded the stable would probably have combined the natural odors of farm animals with the scent of rotting hay, and—how do I say this delicately?—manure. Probably not the most sanitary conditions in which to introduce a child into the world. It was probably not very warm in the stable either. Without the furry coverings that kept the animals warm, it was probably a challenge for Mary and

Joseph just to keep from shivering with the penetrating cold. No doubt they were concerned that their child might catch cold in the chilly night air. Hopefully they had packed a few extra blankets for their journey.

And these two young and inexperi-enced parents were probably fright-ened. Left to bring a child into the world without the assistance of a mid-wife, they no doubt considered in their minds all the things that could go wrong and thought through all the sce-narios they might have to face. The cir-cumstances surrounding the pregnancy probably didn't help the situation much either. Although Joseph's mind had been set at ease by a visiting angel, the rest of their

How Our Family Celebrates Christmas

Some friends of ours have an interesting Christmas tradition. They set up their own nativity scene near the fireplace mantle using stuffed animals, dolls, toys, etc. and leave the manger empty. Then, on Christmas morning, the first gift they unwrap is always the "baby Jesus" (a baby doll). They place Him in His manger and take time to pray, thanking God for the best Christmas gift and singing praise to Him before any gifts under the tree are opened.

ANGELA ISAKSON, BOISE, IDAHO

until months or even a few years later.) Nor was there a notice in the *Jerusalem Post* announcing the coming birth. In fact, it is doubtful that much of anybody realized what had taken place that night in Bethlehem. If God had wanted the world to know what was going on, He certainly could have chosen a better company to put together the publicity campaign. Of course the angels were aware of the birth, but nobody except a few shepherds seemed to be aware of the angels. And the shepherds were not exactly highly prized members of Hebrew society. Living together in small groups, away from civilized society for

hometown had not had that advantage. I wonder if people talked? If Mary's virtue was questioned by the neighbors? Perhaps it was almost a relief to have the baby in a location out of town.

When the baby came, there were no VIPs, religious leaders, or local political figures to welcome Him. (Scholars remind us that the wise men didn't visit

months at a time, their manners and demeanor were what you might expect from such circumstances: rough, unpolished, crude. They wore the stigma that sailors used to wear in our culture. Not exactly at the top of your guest list for who you would want hanging around the recovery room after you had given birth.

All in all, we would have to say that the first Christmas was something of a scandal. It just didn't happen the way we would plan it if it was up to us to orchestrate the birth of the Son of God. Shouldn't there have been more fanfare? More comfort and better conditions? Shouldn't the whole thing have been more dignified? Instead of being accompanied by the blaze of trumpets, only the lowing of cattle and bleating of sheep accompanied the cry of the tiny babe.

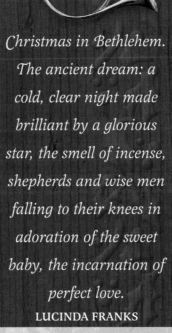

Christmas in Bethlehem. The ancient dream: a cold, clear night made brilliant by a glorious star, the smell of incense, shepherds and wise men falling to their knees in adoration of the sweet baby, the incarnation of perfect love.

LUCINDA FRANKS

No, the scene at the manger was probably not nearly as pretty and tidy as the Renaissance paintings and the Hallmark cards have made it out to be. But neither is real life. Over the years we have romanticized the Christmas story and prettified all the details, ignoring the pain, confusion, and fear which undoubtedly surrounded it. We have removed much of the harsh reality from the Christmas story in the mistaken belief that we need it to be pretty and safe if it is to

Gary Talbott

bring us real comfort. Our lives are difficult enough already. What we really want is to be able to draw a sense of wonder from the story of Christ's birth and some light to give us hope—the hope that our lives can be as simple and peaceful and beautiful as that birth some 2000 years ago in a small town in Judea.

But Christmas isn't just a nice story. The real story of Christmas is not meant merely to inspire positive thoughts, to give us an imaginary sense of peace, or to help us temporarily put away thoughts of our troubles. Christmas is not just about sleigh bells, mistletoe, decorations, and good cheer. It is not just a game we play with ourselves in order to feel better about our life, or a season

How Our Family Celebrates Christmas

Each year there is a gift wrapped under the Christmas tree with the following tag: "To the Nielsons. Love, Abba." Whenever this gift is found in the process of our gift-giving on Christmas Day, it is opened. Inside there is a baby wrapped in a blue cloth and a brief note that says something like: "Here is My greatest gift to you. I want you to remember how much I love you and that I have chosen to come and be with you. Remember in all your celebration, that I have given you the best gift I have to offer." Then there is a brief order of family devotions that might include reading the Christmas story, singing a carol, readings, and prayer. After this time of worship, we return to our gift-giving, having intentionally reminded ourselves about what Christmas is all about and the greatest gift the world has ever known. Finally, someone is given the Abba gift and is responsible to put it together next year to be opened once again with joy and gratitude.

PASTOR JOHN NIELSON,
UPPER MARLBORO, MARYLAND

of the year to try to be extra-nice. After all, what do we do once the season is over—once the needles have fallen from the Christmas tree, the wreaths and greenery have turned brown, the lights have been taken down, and the decorations have all been stored away for another year? Does some of the good cheer disappear once the stores quit playing Christmas carols and the holiday items are placed on a closeout discount table? Why is the transition back to normal life after the holidays sometimes so difficult? Is it that we don't want to let go of the hope of a reality better than our own?

But there is such a reality. That is the continuing message of Christmas. Just as God once entered the world in the form of a baby, so He continues to enter into our world in unexpected and life-changing ways. The real hope of the Christmas story is that God will enter into our own lives in much the same way He did in that manger back in Bethlehem. The circumstances of our lives may not be ideal for his coming and the condition of our hearts may make them seem an inhospitable place for Him. Nevertheless, He comes. Behold, God is with us.

Part of the wonder of the Christmas story is that it can invade our daily life. When we open our hearts to the Lord, we can bring the spirit of Christmas into every day of the year.

He can bring the light of His presence into even the most hopeless and despairing of circumstances. In the rough-and-tumble of our daily lives,

Through the clear, wintry sunshine the bells this morning rang from the fray church tower amid the leafless elms and the red-faced rustic congregation hung on the good man's voice as he spoke of the infant brought forth in a manger... with the story every one was familiar, but on that day...it seemed to all quite new.

FROM THE ALEXANDER SMITH COLLECTION

amid all our fears and failures, the story of Christmas can be lived anew. Christ can be born again in our hearts. His presence can be felt in our lives. And we do not need to pretend that we are full of good cheer when we are hurting. Sometimes the harsh realities of life are the conduit through which the deeper magic of Christmas flows.

God invites you to make the Christmas story a reality in your own life. To make it part of *your* story. He reminds you that you don't have to have all the stalls cleaned out and made perfect for His entry. He will make His home in even the most humble manger or heart.

How Our Family Celebrates Christmas

Because Christmas is Jesus' birthday, we came to the conclusion that gift-giving should be directed toward Him. It did not take us much reading of Scripture to see Jesus' heart for the poor and recognize that we knew others who were in financial need. The best way to give Him a gift was to help someone else instead of spending the money on our own family. I'll never forget the joy of that first time of shopping for a family in our church and the delight they took in the gifts we bought for them. It became a wonderful tradition for us. It is more fulfilling than gift exchanges within our family could be and takes our eyes off ourselves during the Christmas season. It has brought about many interesting conversations in the stores when the children are asked, "What do you want for Christmas?" Instead, for our family, the question is, "What are you giving for Christmas this year?"

JULIE RIEDEL, FRANKLIN, TENNESSEE

A Christmas Meditation

by Michael Card

Just this Christmas it has struck me what a perfect parable the nativity of Jesus was. Choose any single element and you can construct a wonderful lesson. Integrate them all and you will have the basis for understanding your entire life.

In the desperate conditions of the birth we see a parable of our own existence as believers in a world that is determined to make no room for us. They would have us sleep in the stable or worse.

In the coming of the shepherds we can understand our own calling to recognize the outcast and bottom rung of society. Not necessarily because of their own need, but because, as we learn from the shepherds, the foolish and outcast are often the first (and sometimes only) ones to recognize the dignity of Christ, irregardless of the lowly situation of His birth, life, and certainly His death on the cross.

In the Magi we see that, despite what I said above, there is an element hidden within the rich and "intellectual" of this world who will still recognize their hunger and need for Him. Despite the fact that they possess all the world's wisdom, the truly wise still know that there is infinitely more waiting for them than the crumbs that the world's wisdom has to offer.

The nativity as parable, as a moment in history when all that can come together, did come together. A moment when the wise see the wisdom of foolishness, when the outcast come to experience the unqualified acceptance of God, when the world that is determined to shut Him out discovers that He has entered through the back door of history to be born in a manner no one could have predicted. And all this is a parable of our own lives as well. I do not look at the birth of Jesus simply to look selfishly back at myself. But when I do gaze at the Wisdom He is, I invariably discover that the Light is shining back on my own life and making sense out of what made little sense to me before.